DREAMING OF ZEUS

DREAMING OF ZEUS

Lesley Hardy

ISOBAR
PRESS

First published in 2015 by

Isobar Press

14 Isokon Flats, Lawn Road,
London NW3 2XD, United Kingdom
&
Sakura 2-21-23-202, Setagaya-ku,
Tokyo 156-0053, Japan

http://isobarpress.com

ISBN 978-4-907359-09-6

Copyright © Lesley Hardy, 2015
All rights reserved.

The image on page 47 is a reproduction of Figure 1
of *Ars generalis ultima* by Ramon Lull; that on page 55 is from
Arbre de ciència by the same author, printed in Barcelona
in 1505 (*sc.L9695.482ab, Houghton Library, Harvard
University).

*With deepest thanks to Paul Rossiter,
and to Chris Cleary, John Gribble, David Schloss,
and Norio Wada.*

Contents

I

Erik Satie	11
John Cage	13

II

Ohio Pastorale	17
The Leaves	19
Kiyohime	20
Memo	21
The Persephone Experience	23
Dreams of Miss P	25
Saving the World	26
Charm	28
Dreams of Zeus	30

III

Persephone	35
Hephaestus: The Bronze Aphrodite	37
Hera	39
Artemis	41
Persephone: Picking Flowers in a Field	45

IV

Lullian Circle	50
The Moor	56

I

Erik Satie

for Karin Wolff

His pencil flows against the beat of the clock,
and the afternoon's shadows looming over his café table.
He looks up: carriages and passersby in hats and topcoats
stream past the window, and in the café, the cleared tables,
the waiter in his black apron, standing watch.

A brown leaf descends, slowly.
He tells himself:
Despair is a pompous personage
who rushes about in a stiff gray suit,
goatee bristling with outrage at the chirps of sparrows,
a monocled eye snapping about the street
for scraps of cheer to thrash with his umbrella.

He, himself, the Velvet Gentleman,
has no more need of despair.
No, he delights in the homely virtues, the simple joys.
Productivity is enough, thank you,
a few coins for playing his songs on the piano,
and Suzanne's portrait and his on the wall
side by side above the bed they shared
until she went off with her boy and her wagon.

The specter of their union, that orphaned child,
still pads into his orbit now and then.
That night, during his set,
it appears among the noisy tables
and gusts of cigar smoke, stares at him at the piano
as though he were a building with the wrong address,
and then it fades away.

The mirror behind the bar shows a shadow of
the black-gray ether lingering about him these days.
Fog smothering a sunburst –
a permanent state, he supposes, but no hindrance
to the music engine humming inside him.

'Nuance!' or some other improving directive
he would shout through the fog to his acolytes, if he had any,
assume a foreign accent, perhaps, urge them
to put aside their scores and pencils, unfurrow their brows,
and imagine themselves dogs in a moonlit vineyard,
yapping, kicking up dirt,
at play among the grapes and leaves.

He makes it home on foot
in the small hours. A beggar
totters from an empty doorway,
hands open, as if holding
the answer to a prayer.

John Cage

> 'Which of the seven modes, if we take as modes the
> seven scales beginning on white notes and remaining
> on white notes, which of those am I using?'

Horns blare outside the window framing
the composer's Roman-emperor face and hair.
He pets the kitten.
'And when they finally understand, they say,
It's just sounds, then?
It doesn't have to mean anything?'

Shall we walk in the garden that is
an ode to emptiness, to possibility,
rocks raked, clean, the air a screen
for the weather?

In some other garden, under a shower of leaves,
hooded monks walk in a row.
Above the crunch
of footsteps, wing flaps sound.

Wind rushes through the abbey window.
Manuscript pages stacked on the desk
take flight, swirl, land
where they land.

II

Ohio Pastorale

It was efficient, perhaps virtuous –
in a small-town, Protestant way –
to combine babysitting with lawn care.
Retired from the grocery, Mr C pulled up weeds
and threw them, roots dangling, into a black garbage bag.

In summer the boys were mostly shirtless.
Showing their tanned, bony shoulders,
they dug in the sandbox or played ball on the lawn.
The girls were told to play dolls in the shade,
or in the living room on the circle rug,
with its ribbon of cloth coiling from the center out
while Mrs C, in her polished old lady shoes
and starched dress, rocked back and forth in her chair.

But if you did play in the sandbox you had to clean up,
and maybe Mr C helped you in the basement,
down the dark staircase,
the dim room with the small window showing grass,
the sink with the hose, the sandy water
foaming about your feet on the chilly floor and
swirling down the drain.

Sometimes he helped even if you did not play in the sandbox.
In the far, shaded corner of the dining room,
in view of Mrs C's rocking shadow,
he breathed coffee with cream into your ear
and whispered, 'Keep quiet, now,'
fixed whatever was bad under your clothes
and then neatened you with a friendly pat.

Some went back to diapers, and silence or wailing.
Others showed no ill effects.
Nothing was said, but other arrangements were made.
The house and lawn emptied of children.

Afterwards Mrs C swung on the porch swing,
back and forth. Breaking from his yard work,
Mr C gripped the pickets of the high white fence
and faced the street with a hungry look.

Passersby were reflected in his sunglasses.
'How's it going, Mr C?'

'Weeds taking over the lawn,' he said, showing teeth.

The Leaves

Some evenings when I get home early,
I hear a sound that reminds me
of a visitor from long ago,
but it's the neighbor brushing against my door
on his way from the elevator –
that, or the wind.

Or the leaves.
Later, after the traffic has quieted
and the buildings are dark, I go to the balcony
and watch them float down
through dust motes white from the streetlight.
With transparent skins and exposed veins,
they turn with the grace of dancers,
coming to rest on the pavement,
bare and delicate, silver under the light,
until the wind scatters them away.

Kiyohime

(from a story in Japanese puppet theater)

Your boat vanished in the darkness.
The sound of your oars faded in the water's silence.

I stand on the porch and watch the rain,
serenely, as though you were forgotten,
walk along the garden paths,
showing a glimpse of white fingers under my sleeve,
and pause,
my head turned in the manner of a ceramic
displayed for its perfection.

The pillow kept the shape of your head
long after the door slid closed behind you.
Soon the tree roots will claw deeper, into cold earth,
and feed on the sunken rot of leaves and dead insects.

Wrapped in my cloak
with my sharp teeth and dry eyes,
I will walk among the townspeople as though I were a stranger
and wander the icy banks of the river.

When spring comes, the currents
will draw the pins from my hair and loosen my robes,
pull me to the other side and lay me gently on the shore.
I will find you there,
where the grass grows wild,
and the trees stand black and desolate
in the rain.

Memo

One may want to be a poet,
but not like those poets
in re-runs of black and white documentaries
filmed when neurosis was in flower
and smoking and drinking almost Holy Communion –

those poets with their bad skin and ink-stained fingernails,
who sat with their notebooks in bleak diners and various
                                                      stripes of bars,
or at a typewriter in a smoky, single-bulb room,
who conducted mumbled readings to sparse, coughing audiences,
and once in a while, sporting a cigarette and a booze-
                                                splattered jacket,
went out for air on the city's sidewalks.

Today, long after the kingdom of Neurosis was abolished,
the term expunged from the diagnostic canon,
and DT's, cigarette breath, and coffee-stained teeth deemed passé,
a dwindling corps of refuseniks still wanders the landscape.

Blinking at sunlight, they brandish
their self-published volumes and declaim their verse at traffic.
Their dime-tip diners are long gone, and when
they heave their incommodious personalities
and threadbare wallets into mid-tier restaurants,
the maitre d's heart turns cold.

No, not the ideal lunch clientele or professional success model,
but even so, it might be instructive, or at least cautionary,
to have lunch with such a poet.

Alternatively, one might be a poet –
although that might mean shortening lunch
and trying to write some poems.

Perhaps I will try it.

And if I am ever afforded the honor
of declaiming my work in a widely unseen documentary,
with my neuroses – though long past their expiration date –
panting excitedly like puppies,
I will fall to my knees and cry,
'Thank you, God!'

And then move on to prose.

The Persephone Experience

Every girl has it, again and again.
Down to the Underworld for some character-building,
then back up to meadowland.

There are reasons – her man left,
the Suzy Homemaker number didn't work out,
the company folded,
she lost it all in the equities crash,
or just took too many wrong turns –
so instead of having it all, or having some of it,
she doesn't have any of it.

And then one day
there is no more time: her date of birth
has wiped her off the field,
and whether in the employment world
or the social world, or even the Underworld,
she is forever 'free to go' – that is,
to her own private-label underworld.

And it ain't Hawaii –
but what the hell,
if she still has a kitchen,
she is free to bang some pans around,
bust up a toaster, whatever it takes,
free to use what she's got
to make a dish, and then another and another,
down-payments on her Golden Years,
free to serve them all up to the indifferent world
and wait for Notice of Receipt,

of which the sum will be commensurate
with what she is deemed to have given,
which will be Nothing –

Nothing, snapping at her feet like a restless dog.

Dreams of Miss P

Years ago, the new trainees in the Trust Department
were told about Miss P,
the client who 'lost it' in Conference Room 5
one Friday afternoon. Her tears splattering the table,
she screamed at her trust officers, screamed
as she had already screamed away men, families, houses.

After that she trailed off the elevator each month
in the same blue skirt,
waited in her usual chair for her check,
flicked cigarette ash into the shiny receptacle
and blew out smoke.

I saw her in a dream before she died.
Through a fist-sized opening in my cell wall
I peered into a studio with shimmering windows,
and dancers – not bodies but radiant outlines
trailing streams of silver light.

A man in a grimy kitchen
shouted at me through my cell bars.
Shadowy beings skittered about him.
She, in her blue skirt, appeared at his side. Her eyes
filled my field of vision, and I spun away from her,
back to that studio pulsing with light,
where I ached to belong and swore to myself I belonged.

In another dream she was sitting in a garden
in a stream of sunlight,
her face set fiercely against the sky,
while all around her flowers sprang forth
releasing their insistent perfumes.

Saving the World

Up from hell
the outline of a gnashing, fire-spitting beast
boils around the city.
Traffic snarls. Knives flash on the sidewalk.
Smoke churns from a wrecked car.

A stranger in an old suit, thin tie and fedora,
straight out of Philip K. Dick,
steps in to inform you of your status
in the clash between good and evil.
It is your mission to restore the world, he says.

Still dressed for the office, your shoes coated with dust,
you stumble about in over-bright nature scenes,
and can't remember why you are there.
Choleric bursts of orange and red,
from a typewriter punched by an SF writer's meth-fueled fingers,
gust into the narrative.

But now you have lost the plot.
The future – and *your* future – have slipped away.

The sky darkens. You see the stranger
in his glowing psychic control tower.
He stares into you, makes his assessment, and turns away.
The tower dissolves from view.
The mission has been transferred
from your hands to those of a more worthy agent,
and you are abandoned to your own mediocrity.

The beast fades away.
The sun comes up on the city.
The fires of hell burning low, the chaos is at bay for now.

The typewriter is silent.

You end the dream an exile from self-belief, a wanderer,
your companions the coded birdsong in your ears,
the whispering leaves,
the untrustable beauty of trees.

Charm

> *When a friend advised using charm to help me deal with a difficult bureaucrat, I thought, in a mental voice that could have been my father's: charm is a risky gambit for a Calvinist from the American mid-west.*

And so is music. Not perhaps to the real Calvin,
who permitted the Psalms – but only the Psalms – to be sung,
but to the spiritual children of that other Calvin,
that black-robed cleric snarling in the popular imagination,
vivid as Lucifer, whose pulpit excoriations
stormed through the cosmos, and by their force
jangled the stars and caused the spinning spheres to tremble.

My father wore a black suit
to perform his earthly callings of musician and teacher.
His clarinet stood next to his chair at home,
and he often took it up and silently worked out fingerings.

Childhood polio made him walk with a limp,
but not when he strode onto the stage:
his shadow swept the curtain
like the wings of an enraged celestial prosecutor,
and he was a stranger, a priest
sparked with power to draw down music
and deliver it into the auditorium's darkness
through his clarinet.

His children were sometimes sent to Sunday School,
taught by women in bright dresses. At home
he admired our crayon drawings, listened to our songs,
and made no mention of hellfire or the elect.

Calvin, the real one, lost his voice at the end
yet faithfully hobbled in to the pews. My father
lost control of a finger in his forties.
Nerve damage. His clarinet disappeared.
He took up cooking, put away the black
and started wearing colors, like the rest of us.

A few years after he died I dreamed about us
in the living room of the final family home.
A gray prehistoric animal the length of a tennis racket
ran wildly about, then clamped its snout on my foot.
My father looked up from his reading.
'Well, Les, it looks like you've got
a prehistoric animal stuck on your foot.'

Well, yes, there is always a catch if you're Presbyterian.
But at least I did get to see him again,
in his black suit and blue chair with his clarinet,
and his stack of books in the circle of lamplight,
and a representative of a defunct, perhaps mythological species
did spring to life in our living room
and later ushered me to the next dream,
into an upstairs room, an amalgam of bedrooms from childhood,
a Hollywood-style night-fall glimmering outside the window
while I swung in circles
on a star-lit rope let down from above.

Dreams of Zeus

You lounged in the shade, in a white linen suit,
holding an armful of flowers
with drops of water sparkling on their petals,
while I clicked by in the sun's glare with briefcase and files.

In another dream, behind a door
cracked open to a room lit by the evening sky,
you were an old man in black.
Your voice came to me from the shadows.
Your eyelids were lowered in deference
not to me, but to the sheen that drenches
a young woman's limbs and hair like moonlight,
returning to me as I stepped into that room.

From time to time you materialize in the waking world.
Flashing cufflinks and dental work,
swatting aside maxims from the self-help canon,
trailing cigarette ash and the fumes of cognac and cologne
through modest, abstemious rooms,
you conquer and then depart,
leaving the mortals to clear the wreckage.

Each time, awakened by you,
I went forth in your service, and each time fell,
cut down by my own assassins –
the drab-tongued functionary at her desk,
or the aging naïf choked on small-town earnestness,
or some other dreary persona circulating in my repertoire.
Each time brought back to my earthly proportions, tangled
in them like a parachutist in her ropes,
I got up and went about my business,

but still watched and listened
for signs of you – and sometimes
felt a shiver at the back of my neck.

In the last dream
I watched you float by on a barge of clouds.
Your gaze passed over mine,
and then the sky took you away.

That leaves me
in this small high-rise apartment,
the street below filling with taxis and office workers,
daylight moving off the buildings and fading through the trees
as I linger, with a few plants I tend, on my balcony,
where I might watch the lights tonight,
and the stars if there are any,
and in the morning choose a sprig for the vase.

III

Persephone

I dropped a flower in the meadow.

The maidens found it and took my mother there,
and she heard my cries from the kingdom.

She fell to her knees and beat the grass.
The maidens pulled her up, wiped the dirt
from her cheek, and led her home.

Bathed, dressed in finery, she went to the tribunal,
down the long gleaming corridor
to the men watching in silence from their thrones,
and threw herself down before them.

The maidens stand watch over the meadow.
I know how the sunlight glints in their hair.
At night my mother paces above my cavern,
her fists white in the moonlight.

But I have listened to the voice of my captor
speaking to me from the other side of the doorway.
I have warmed myself at the cavern's fires
and watched my face in fascination in the mirror.
I have eaten from bowls brought in by servants,
smelled the bitter powders in my cup, and drunk.

I slept while desolation shrouded the earth.
The sky was stripped of brightness.
The rivers' flows were stopped, meadows and trees
scraped bare by my mother's grief.

Crows pick at the meadow's frost.
The maidens' hair is shorn and gray.
Their faces are lined. The hems
of their black gowns flap about their ankles.
They watch without speaking as
my mother paces above my cavern
with her torn gown and her hair grown wild.

She will close her eyes and see
the King of Death coming to her.
His robes will flare in the whipping wind,
ice shatter beneath him as he crosses the river.
She will open her eyes to the meadow full of flowers
as I step upon it, mouth wet with fruit.

Hephaestus: The Bronze Aphrodite

Hammers pound metal.
Gusts of smoke
burst from the forge
and billow about the workers' arms.

The Master's shadow
moves over the rows of sculptors wielding hammers.
His limp scrapes a path through cinders and copper rakings.

He pauses to watch the smiths pound hot iron.
Clasped in tongs, scattering sparks,
the burning metal casts light on the anvils –
the same rose light that tints his garden pool at dusk
and shines through his banquet-room candle shades
onto the face of his wife.

He withdraws to a passageway, as he sometimes does.
The blackness soaks into him.
He thinks of his wife – her silhouette on the balcony
looking out at the clouds streaked with moonlight –
and of himself drawing up beside her,
careful to give her notice with a rustle of his sleeve.
Eyes shadowed by darkness, she turns her face toward him.
He senses the warm pulse of her.
The perfumes of their garden stir.
The breeze cools his hand on the railing
about to reach over toward her.
And then, almost imperceptibly, she pulls away.

He limps back through the workshop,
through the pounding and shouts,
the waves of heat and smoke,
wipes his hands and straightens his smock,
faces the bronze laid out for him on the table
and takes up his hammer.

Hera

About the worst that can happen these days
is poor service at the tea salon. But that is unlikely,
for the distinction of the customer is signaled
by the black car she emerges from at the door,
the tailored dinner suit, the jeweled watch catching the light
when she lifts her cup.

Even so, she is still susceptible to her memories,
now stirred by the window view from her banquette –
a young woman scrambling past with packages and a stroller,
another putting away her phone with an expression of defeat,
another shining on the arm of a silver-haired man –
and she scans back over the years of strife:
babies pushed through her womb
(allies, enemies, defectives, always a gamble),
battles to defend her home against the treachery of women,
doomed campaigns for her place
in her husband's esteem and in his bed.

Those years stripped the softness from her,
fashioned her voice into a harsh instrument,
scraped everything out of her but fear and rage.
They cast her into the barren grove and anointed her with failure.
And then they made her effective.

Wild-eyed shrieking in the street,
fingernails clawing for blood, snake venom in fruit –
all such vain tactics were exiled
as though they were misshapen children.
Her arena shifted, to quiet rooms of power.

Enemies were dis-armed, alliances forged.
She gave and raised money, spoke in cultured tones
in defense of family and home.
The whispers that she was nothing
without her husband's power faded away.
Treasure piled in the vaults.
The people bowed down to her
as though she were an effigy paraded on a litter.

Young men in dinner jackets march past the banquette
and try to catch her eye. Some women
would choose one or another, put him in some decent cufflinks
and a better apartment. But why bother?

Family will survive, as hers did, stagger forward
like a team of oxen in plowing season.
Home, battered, yet triumphant, will fulfill its mission.
That is enough. She will glide along the streets in her black car
and lean back on her cushions, behind the smoked glass.

Artemis

1

Sunlight on a beetle's eye.

Birdsong.
A chipmunk scampers along a branch.
Nearby, shrieks from the girls.
One, legs smeared by bark, bustles up a tree

He has filmed them from afar
and captured them in stills –
mid-chase, with hair flying,
or with stained mouths and fists at the berry patch,
or a girl shivering in the bathing stream,
mouth open in a squeal,
hands raised under a cascade of splashes.

A destiny has long claimed him, sequestered him
to low-register jobs and a dingy apartment.
It has bestowed on him the cunning to avoid chatroom bait,
the patience to wait out the indignities of his worldly station,
the self-command to watch and to plan.
It has empowered him to inflict his healing wound.
He marches forward in its service.

2

The setting sun flashes
between the branches of the cypress.
Its shadow looms over the clearing.

At day's end the girls return
to take their places under its branches.
If one needs comforting
she stretches her arms around its trunk and rests
a cheek on its bark. At night
its soft needles cushion them in their sleep.

3

He has pushed through the forest to the edge of the clearing
and gazed upon the cypress crowned by moonlight.
He has watched the sleeping girls, their gowns silver
in the pale light, noted the soft catches in their breaths.

He has waited for someone,
conjured in his mind her wild-haired outline
alert and silent in the darkness.
He will bow down to her. Stand guard as she sleeps.
In the afternoon heat, he will cool the air about her
with a fan of blossoms. In time
she will uncover for him the depth of her aloneness.
He will wipe her tears and, if permitted, smooth her hair.

Unlike those who cuddle first,
and say, 'You're special,' and then won't stop,
he will always stop. Until
it is time to escort her forward, to teach her fear and pain,
time to enshrine her, in the aftermath of
that moment of advancement and humiliation,
in his lens.

4

He goes back in daylight.
In the distance the girls shriek at their games.

She appears among the trees.
Her green-brown eyes, impersonal as electric lights,
are trained, across the expanse of forest, on him.
He notes the hand holding the bow,
the arrows strapped to her tunic,
the row of silent hounds poised nearby,
and he takes a step toward her.

Red shatters his shirt.
Framed by sun-splattered leaves, he staggers.
Barking hounds shoot towards him.

He is buried now, among the others.
Roots coil about the old bones.
The red on the grass was his brief memorial,
startling as a girl's first blood.

5

In the evenings, the girls sit under the cypress
and braid each other's hair. In the shadows
the beauty of each face, veiled in perpetual girlhood,
glimpses out like an animal from behind a leaf.
Some pull away and climb to the upper branches.
On silent perches they watch the stars,
each glittering in its own distant splendor.

6

Her feet skim the ground.
Loyal hounds pound behind her,
breath hot on her legs,
shreds of leaf scattered in their wake,
flashes of daylight, a blur of branches –

through the forest, a rush of air.

Persephone: Picking Flowers in a Field

You sense someone watching and look back
to see a glimmer under the trees.

Later you will remember a snake
fleeing, and the birds' silence.

The ground snaps open.
A hand snatches you from behind,

drags you deep underground
and hurls you onto a throne of rocks.

A voice rumbling up from the furnace
in the center of the earth names you Queen.

And you *are* Queen –
of ovens flaring in darkness,

of cavern walls flickering in and out of view
and the dropped flowers at your feet,

Queen of buried black promenades
that you will learn to walk with ease,

of grand stone and metal gardens
you will view with an expert eye.

Someone regards you from the doorway,
not unkindly.

And you become the figure painted
on smooth clay vessels, the Consort

seated on a divan, profile
lit by firelight, gazing up at her King.

Above, women wail for their lost powers.
They beat on closed doors and claw their hair.

Their black shawls trail behind them
over windswept fields of yellow grass.

One day, in your spring gown,
with untroubled eyes and smooth hair

you will reappear in a field of flowers
and stoop to pick some, not looking back.

IV

Majorca 1229–1315

Mostly under Islamic rule since 902, Majorca was conquered by James I of Aragon in late 1229–30. Many Moors escaped to the mountains or by sea, while numerous others were killed. After three months the Islamic leader, Abu Yayah, surrendered, and the remaining Moors lost their status, property and former way of life.

Ramon Lull (or Llull, 1232–c. 1315) was born into a noble family who, immediately after the invasion, had come from Catalonia to the new Kingdom of Majorca as colonists. As a courtier he was a prolific writer of poetry and philosophy and engaged in a life of pleasure, but after a conversion experience he dedicated himself to Christianity. On the last of his missions to North Africa he was attacked by a stone-throwing crowd while he preached. He is thought to have died from those wounds, but the place of his death is unknown: some reports have him dying in North Africa, some on a Genoese merchant ship en route to Majorca, and still others at home. At least one account places his death in his olive grove.

As an aid to converting non-Christians, Lull designed a prototype knowledge-generating device, which became known, through its influence on Leibniz, as a precursor to the computer. Lull's early romantic novel Blanquerna *(1283) is generally regarded as the first major work in Catalan literature, but in all he wrote more than 250 works in Catalan, Latin and Arabic, the most famous being* Ars generalis ultima *(The Ultimate General Art, 1305), which outlines the religious, philosophical and methodological thinking that lay behind the invention of his device.*

Lullian Circle

1

A storm of whirling alphabet letters.
So much Truth to configure.

The ship shudders against a wave.
His eyes open to the gray ceiling and then close.

2

A row of cassocks.
Faces blotted out in a dazzle of sunlight.

On the lecture table lay his Circle:
two disks of heavy paper (the inner smaller than the outer)
connected at their centers by a silver-tipped pin,
the circumference of the outer disk
just larger than a serving plate.

Next to it, a leather-bound companion volume, the Index.

It had come to him in his olive grove,
with his back hot against a tree.
What was that warmth but life itself,
the breath of God pulsing up through roots and trunk
to the leaves and olives that dangled before his eyes,
and then drifted out as scent.
It sprang into his mind: a device as elegant as a tree –
a knowledge machine, an analogue of God.

He held up the Circle for the Pope's men to see.
Inscribed on the inner disk's rim were the Virtues:
'Goodness, Greatness, Duration, Power, Wisdom,
Will, Virtue, Truth and Glory,' he recited,
'The sum of God in man's words.'

On the outer disk's rim were letters,
explained in the Index, he told them,
where each letter can be paired with any Virtue
for examination of God's nature,
to lead the Infidel, by reason, to Truth.

He turned the inner disk.
The rustle of paper sounded uncouthly in the grand hall,
like an animal waking on a bed of leaves.
It stopped at Duration:
'God's eternity, and man's echo of that sublimity.'
He set the outer disk at D.

The line of cassocks blurred into a black barricade.

'What virtue pairs with D? What vice? What quality?'
Snapping the pages of the Index for drama,
he found D, although he could have spoken it by heart:
'The corresponding virtue is Fortitude, the vice Lust –
and the quality? Contrareity.'

He did not tell them how Lust
had crowded out the pure in him,
driven him with ruthless Fortitude
to vainglorious conquest of women,
to worthless songs and poems and other licentious things.

Holding the Index, he sighed.
Ah, the Duration of his pride, his passions –
yet in sin he had remained a tourist.
Experience had barely ruffled
the icy garden of his solitude.

He did not tell them how Lust,
as his guide and teacher,
had revealed to him, in the fulfillment of desire,
the banality of his aspirations,
and thus delivered him at last
to the Contrareity of all such vanity – that is, to Truth.

3

Truth had once been a Lady,
muse to his treatises on love's arts.
When they passed in the corridor,
in a dreamlike passacaglia,
her velvet shadow had brushed across him
like a hand drawn over the strings of a harp.

The rustle of her skirts had faded,
and in the silence he had known
the emptiness of his unredeemed soul.

As though stepping
through picture frames into court dances, banquets,
and gardens under shuttered windows,
he had sought substitutes for her among the sex.

Yet after each conquest, the old chill –
and in his mind's eye the gold train of her gown
vanishing through a far-off doorway.

Until one night
the voice of the Lord had called to him
and the doorway had filled with radiance.

4

'For D the realm is Heaven,
and the question, *Of What?*' He would not presume
to speak to the Pope's men of Heaven. Instead, he told them
Of What his life had consisted in the Lord's service:

Ocean voyages to the lands
of the Infidel, treks and wagon rides over rough hills,
sermons preached on city streets,
his Lord's Virtues shouted into markets and courtyards,
demonstrations of his Circle in shaded gardens,
months in jail, chained to a post for blasphemy –
all that had seemed to pass in the span of a season –
all occasions for praise.

The blank faces, now visible in the setting sun,
signaled him to look elsewhere
for the coin to fund his next mission.

5

One morning he was preaching on a square in Tunis.
A rock knocked the words out of his throat. Another
glided through the sunlight and struck his chest.

A fleet of rocks floated toward him.
He drifted downward.
The shouts of his assailants dimmed as in a wave.
Their faces bobbed in the distance like specks of foam.
He called God's blessing upon them,
and upon his own soul.

6

'Majorca ahead!' someone shouts.
The gray ceiling dissolves, the rush of wind and cloud,
a golden doorway.

The trees stand in clusters near his villa in Majorca
arms raised
dispensing the scent of olive blossoms.

The Moor

Majorca, c. 1300

Waves drop shells and fish bones at my feet.
The sky turns from black to gray.
The gulls cry out. Fishing boats pull in to shore
with their mounds of bloody catch.

The sun comes up like a gong raised slowly
for a king's inspection.

I am black, but in my robe
a white pillar gliding through the market
like a statue on a barge.
The crowd makes way as I pass through.
The air smells of heat and fruit and spices.
Crows caw over the shop owners' cries.

Under a haze of flies at the meat vendor's
strips of goat flesh drape the stand.
A bead of blood
drops to the ground.

In a wave of dust the market tears down for the day
and the carts plod off.
The square empties.
Window shades draw down against the sun.

At last, evening shadows fill the courtyards and doorways.
The smell of saffron drifts from a kitchen window.
Around the corner a man takes up a song.
I reach up and pluck a leaf,
draw it over my cheek,
pull its smell into my nostrils,
crush it to my neck.

Long ago my passions left me
like pearls sliding off their thread.

And on this shore again,
I see no ship waiting in those black waters.
The stars send me no prophecy,
and the waves fling their jewels at my feet.

www.ingramcontent.com/pod-product-compliance
Lightning Source LLC
Chambersburg PA
CBHW031216090426
42736CB00009B/944